PAGE 16

M000023245

PAGE 6

# CONTENT

## Beginner

## Easy

PAGE 12

PAGE 21

## Intermediate

PAGE 10

# YOGA Bag

Rose Callahan

## YOU'LL NEED:

### YARN
1¾oz/50g, 180yd/160m of any fingering weight wool yarn each in silver (MC), purple (A), lilac (B), lime green (C), navy blue (D), deep purple (E), blue (F), and blue multi (G)

### NEEDLES
One pair size 3 (3.25mm) needles *or size to obtain gauge*

## SIZE
One size.

## MEASUREMENTS
**Circumference** 14"/35.5cm
**Length** 26"/66cm

## GAUGE
33 sts and 35 rows to 4"/10cm in chevron pattern.
*Take time to check gauge.*

## STITCH GLOSSARY
**Stripe Pattern**
14 rows A, 14 rows B, 14 rows MC, 4 rows C, 4 rows MC, 14 rows C, 14 rows G, 14 rows D, 4 rows D, 4 rows B, 4 rows D, 4 rows B, 14 rows D, 14 rows E, 4 rows A, 4 rows E, 14 rows A, 14 rows B, 14 rows F, 4 rows A, 4 rows F, 14 rows A, 14 rows G.
These 222 rows make up the Stripe Pat.
**Chevron Pattern** (multiple of 16 sts plus 3)
**Row 1** Purl. **Row 2** K1, *k1, k2tog, k5, M1, k1, M1, k5, SKP; rep from * to last 2 sts, k2. Rep rows 1 and 2 for chevron pat.

## BAG
With MC, cast on 115 sts.
**Row 1 (WS)** Purl. **Row 2** K1, *k1, M1, k5, SKP, k1, k2tog, k5, M1; rep from * to last 2 sts, k2.
Rep last 2 rows 3 times more, then work row 1 once more. **Next (turning ridge) row (RS)** Purl. Work in chevron pat for 5 rows. Work in stripe pat and cont chevron pat for 222 rows of stripe pat. **Next (WS) row** With MC, Purl. **Next (turning ridge) row (RS)** Purl.
**Shape Bottom**
**Row 1 and all WS rows** Purl. **Row 2 (RS)** K1, *k1, k2tog, k5, M1, k1, M1, k5, SKP; rep from * to last 2 sts, k2.
**Row 4** K1, *k1, k2tog, k11, SKP; rep from * to last 2 sts, k2—101 sts.
**Row 6** K1, *k1, k2tog, k4, M1, k1, M1, k4, SKP; rep from * to last 2 sts, k2. **Row 8** K1, *k1, k2tog, k9, SKP, rep from * to last 2 sts, k2—87 sts. **Row 10** K1, *k1, k2tog, k3, M1, k1, M1, k3, SKP; rep from * to last 2 sts, k2.
**Row 12** K1, *k1, k2tog, k7, SKP; rep from * to last 2 sts, k2—73 sts.
**Row 14** K1, *k1, k2tog, k2, M1, k1, M1, k2, SKP; rep from * to last 2 sts, k2. **Row 16** K1, *k1, k2tog, SKP; rep from * to last 2 sts, k2.
**Row 18** K1, *k2tog; rep from * to end of row. Cut yarn with 12"/30.5cm tail, thread through rem sts and cinch tightly to close.

## FINISHING
Block piece to measurements. Sew seam, leaving 1"/2.5cm open before turning ridge (for drawstring). Fold top at turning ridge and slip st in place to WS.

**Drawstring**
Using 8 strands of yarn held together, make a twisted cord with a finished length of approx 66"/167.5cm. Thread through upper casing and secure both ends together at seam at start of bottom shaping.

# CUP Sleeve/Cozy

## YOU'LL NEED:

### YARN
1¾oz/50g, 110yd/100m of any worsted weight variegated wool yarn

### NEEDLES
One set (4) size 6 (4mm) double-pointed needles (dpns) *or size to obtain gauge*

### ADDITIONAL MATERIALS
Cable needle (cn)
Stitch marker

## SIZES
Sized for average 12 (16) oz take-out coffee cup. Sleeve fits multiple sized cups. Shown on left in picture.

## MEASUREMENTS
**For cozy**
**Lower circumference** 8"/20.5cm
**Upper circumference** 10 (10½)"/25.5 (26.5) cm
**Length** 3 (4)"/7.5 (10)cm
**For sleeve**
**Lower circumference** 9"/23cm
**Upper circumference** 11"/28cm
**Length** 3½"/9cm

## GAUGE
24 sts and 32 rows to 4"/10cm over St st using size 6 (4mm) needles.
*Take time to check gauge.*

## STITCH GLOSSARY
**4-st RC** Sl 2 sts to cn and hold to *back*, k2, k2 from cn.
**4-st LC** Sl 2 sts to cn and hold to *front*, k2, k2 from cn.
**Cable pattern**
**Rnd 1** K2, 4-st LC, p to marker, 4-st RC, k2, p to end of dpn.
**Rnd 2** K6, p to marker, k6, p to end of dpn.
**Rnd 3** 4-st RC, K2, p to marker, k2, 4-st LC, p to end of dpn.
**Rnd 4** K6, p to marker, k6, p to end of dpn.
Rep rnds 1-4 for cable pat.

## CUP COZY
Cast on 6 sts. Distribute evenly over 3 dpns. Place marker (pm) for beg of rnd and join being careful not to twist sts.
**Rnd 1** [Kfb] 6 times—12 sts.
**Rnd 2** Knit.
**Rnd 3 (inc)** [K1, kfb, k to last 2 sts of dpn, kfb, k1] 3 times—18 sts.
Rep rnds 2 and 3 five times more—48 sts.
**Beg cable pat**
**Set-up rnd** [K6, p2, pm, k6, p2] 3 times. Work rnds 1-4 of cable pat once, then rnds 1-3 once more.
**Inc rnd 1** [K6, kfb, p to marker, k6, kfb, p to end of dpn] 3 times—54 sts. Work 7 rnds in cable pat as established.
**Inc rnd 2** [K6, kfb, p to marker, k6, p to dpn end) 3 times around—57 sts. Work 7 rnds in cable pat as established.
**Inc rnd 3** [K6, p to marker, k6, kfb, p to end of dpn] 3 times—60 sts.
**For 16 oz size only**
Work 7 rnds in cable pat as established. Rep inc rnd 2—63 sts.
**For both sizes**
Bind off purlwise.

## CUP SLEEVE
Cast on 54 sts, and distribute evenly over 3 dpns. PM for beg of rnd and join, being careful not to twist sts.
**Set-up rnd** [K6, p3, pm, k6, p3] 3 times. Work rnds 1-4 of cable pat, then rep rnds 1-3 once more.
**Next (inc) rnd** [K6, kfb, p to marker, k6, kfb, p to end of dpn] 3 times—60 sts. Work 7 rnds in cable pat as established.
**Next (inc) rnd** [K6, kfb, p to marker, k6, p to end of dpn] 3 times—63 sts. Work 7 rnds in cable pat as established.
**Next (inc) rnd** [K6, p to marker, k6, kfb, p to end of dpn] 3 times—66 sts. Bind off purlwise.

# CHUNKY Cowl

## YOU'LL NEED:

### YARN (6)
3½oz/100g, 130yd/120m of any super-bulky weight wool blend yarn

### NEEDLES
One pair size 13 (9mm) needles or *size to obtain gauge*
One extra size 13 (9mm) needle (for 3-needle bind-off)

### ADDITIONAL MATERIALS
Size J/10 (6mm) crochet hook and scrap yarn (for provisional cast on)
Cable needle (cn)

## SIZE
One size. Sized for adult woman.

## MEASUREMENTS
Approximately 11½ x 22"/29 x 56cm

## GAUGE
9½ sts and 13 rows to 4"/10cm over St st, using size 13 (9mm) needles.
*Take time to check gauge.*

## STITCH GLOSSARY
**6-st LC** Slip 3 sts to cn and hold to *front*, k3, k3 from cn.

## SPECIAL TECHNIQUES
**Provisional cast on**
Using scrap yarn and crochet hook, chain the number of sts to cast on plus a few extra. Cut a tail and pull the tail through the last chain. With knitting needle and yarn for project, pick up and knit the stated number of sts through the "purl bumps" on the back of the chain. To remove waste chain, pull out the tail from the last crochet stitch. Gently and slowly pull on the tail to unravel the crochet stitches, carefully placing each released knit stitch on a needle.

**3-Needle Bind-Off**
**1** Hold right sides of pieces together on two needles. Insert third needle knitwise into first st of each needle, and wrap yarn knitwise.
**2** Knit these two sts together, and slip them off the needles. *Knit the next two sts together in the same manner.
**3** Slip first st on 3rd needle over 2nd st and off needle. Rep from * in step 2 across row until all sts are bound off.

## COWL
Using provisional cast on, cast on 28 sts.
**Begin chart**
With size 13 (9mm) needles, work rows 1-26 of chart pat 3 times.

## FINISHING
**Next row** Carefully remove crochet chain and place sts on extra needle. Join ends of cowl tog using 3-needle bind-off.

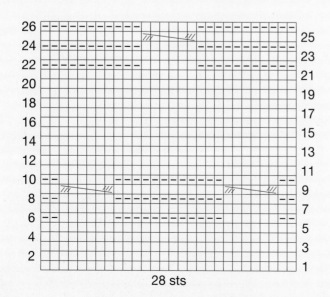

28 sts

## STITCH KEY

☐ k on RS, p on WS

⊟ p on RS, k on WS

⧄⧄⧄ 6-st LC

Rose Callahan

# ALPINE Mittens

## YOU'LL NEED:

### YARN (4)
3½oz/100g, 230yd/210m of any worsted weight wool yarn each in periwinkle (MC) and white (CC)

### NEEDLES
One pair each sizes 6 and 8 (4 and 5mm) needles or *size to obtain gauge*

### ADDITIONAL MATERIALS
Stitch holders
Tapestry needle

## SIZE
One size. Sized for adult woman.

## MEASUREMENTS
**Circumference** 7½"/19cm (above thumb)
**Length** 10"/25.5cm

## GAUGE
20 sts and 26 rows to 4"/10cm over St st using larger needles.
*Take time to check gauge.*

## STITCH GLOSSARY
**Inc 1** K into front and back of next st.
**Corrugated ribbing Row 1 (RS)** *K2 CC, p2 MC; rep from * to end. **Row 2** *K2 MC, p2 CC; rep from * to end. Rep rows 1 and 2 for corrugated ribbing.

## LEFT MITTEN
With smaller needles and CC, cast on 48 sts. Work in corrugated ribbing for 2½"/6.5cm, end with a RS row.

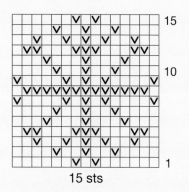

15 sts

### STITCH KEY
☑ Duplicate st (with CC)

**Next (dec) row (WS)** *K2tog, work 10 sts in established pat; rep from * to end of row—44 sts. Change to larger needles and MC. Work in St st (k on RS, p on WS) for 4 rows. **Next (inc) row (RS)** K21, [inc 1] twice, k21—46 sts. Work in St st for 5 rows. **Next (inc) row** K21, inc 1, k2, inc 1, k2 —148 sts. Work in St st for 9 rows. Cut yarn.

### Beg thumb
**Next row (RS)** Sl first 18 sts to a holder, join yarn and k12, sl rem 18 sts to a holder. **Next (inc) row (WS)** Inc 1 st in first st, p5, inc 1, p4, inc 1 st in last st—15 sts. Work in St st for 14 rows. **Next (dec) row (RS)** K1, [k2tog] 7 times—8 sts. **Next (dec) row** [P2tog] 4 times. Cut yarn and draw through rem 4 sts. Fasten off. Sew thumb seam.

### Hand
Rejoin MC to sts from first holder and k18, pick up and k 1 st on both sides of thumb, k18 from 2nd holder–38 sts. Work even until piece measures 9¼"/23.5cm from beg, ending with a WS row.

### Top shaping
**Row 1 (RS)** K1, k2tog, k14, [k2tog] twice, k14, k2tog, k1—34 sts. **Rows 2 and 4** Purl. **Row 3** K1, k2tog, k12, [k2tog] twice, k12, k2tog, k1—30 sts. **Row 5** K1, k2tog, k10, [k2tog] twice, k10, k2tog, k1—26 sts. **Row 6** Purl. Bind off.

## RIGHT MITTEN
Work same as for left mitten.

## FINISHING
With CC and tapestry needle, foll chart and work duplicate st snowflake on back of each mitten. Sew side and top seams.

Rose Callahan

# RIDGED Cowl

*Rose Callahan*

## YOU'LL NEED:

### YARN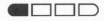
1¾oz/50g, 150yd/140m of any DK weight wool blend yarn

### NEEDLES
One pair size 5 (3.75mm) circular needle, 24"/60cm length *or size to obtain gauge*

### ADDITIONAL MATERIALS
Stitch markers

### SIZE
One size. Sized for adult woman.

### MEASUREMENTS
**Circumference** 26"/66cm
**Height** 9"/23cm

### GAUGE
22 sts and 45 rnds to 4"/10cm over ridge pat.
*Take time to check gauge.*

**Note** This piece is reversible as the ridge pat looks good on either side.

### STITCH GLOSSARY
**Ridge pattern**
Purl 6 rnds, knit 3 rnds.
Rep these 9 rnds for ridge pat.

### COWL
Cast on 146 sts. Taking care not to twist sts, place marker and join for knitting in the round.
Work in ridge pat for 11 reps. Purl 3 more rnds. Bind off loosely purlwise.

# RIBBED Mitts

## YOU'LL NEED:

### YARN
1¾oz/50g, 110yd/100m of any
worsted weight variegated wool

### NEEDLES
One set (5) size 7 (4.5mm) double-
pointed needles (dpns) or *size to
obtain gauge*

### ADDITIONAL MATERIALS
One size H/8 (5mm) crochet hook
Stitch markers

## SIZE
One size. Sized for adult woman.

## MEASUREMENTS
**Circumference** 6½"/16.5cm
**Length** 8"/20.5cm

## GAUGE
24 sts and 30 rows to 4"/10cm over garter rib
using larger needles.
*Take time to check gauge.*

## STITCH GLOSSARY
**Garter rib**
**Rnd 1** *K3, p1, rep from * around. **Rnd 2** Knit.
Rep rnds 1 and 2 for garter rib.

## MITT (make 2)
Cast on 36 sts. Place marker for beg of rnd
and join, being careful not to twist sts. Work in
garter rib until piece measures 6"/15cm from
beg.
**Thumb opening**
**Next rnd** Bind off 5 sts, work to end of rnd.
**Next rnd** Cast on 5 sts, work to end of rnd.
Continue in garter rib for 2"/5cm. Bind off.

## FINISHING
With crochet hook, work one rnd of sc around
thumb opening. Fasten off.

Paul Amato for lvarepresents.com

# POM POM Tea Cozy

Rose Callahan

## YOU'LL NEED:

### YARN (4)
3½oz/100g, 200yd/190m of any worsted weight wool blend yarn each in blue (A), navy (B), and light blue (C)

### NEEDLES
One pair size 8 (5mm) needles or *size to obtain gauge*

### ADDITIONAL MATERIALS
1 dpn a few sizes smaller than straight needle for working tuck

■■□□□

## SIZE
One size.

## MEASUREMENTS
**At widest point** 6"/5.5cm
**At narrowest point** 3"/7.5cm
**Length** 26"/66cm

## GAUGE
20 sts and 24 rows to 4"/10cm over St st using size 8 (5mm) needles.
*Take time to check gauge.*

## STITCH GLOSSARY
**Tuck pattern**
Purl one row on WS.
**Next row (RS)** K 1, k2tog, yo, k to end.
Work 9 rows in St st (K on RS, P on WS).
**Tuck row (RS)** With dpn and purl side facing you, pick up 33 sts from the row just above the yo. Holding the dpn and straight needle parallel so fabric is folded with purl sides together, *k2tog taking 1 st from front needle and 1 st from back needle; repeat from * until all sts are worked.

## TEA COZY
With A, cast on 33 sts and knit one row. Work in Tuck Pat for one repeat. Change color. Work 13 repeats of tuck pat, changing color for each repeat as follows: B, A, C, A, B, A, C, A, B, A, C, A, B. When last repeat has been worked, make handle opening.

## Handle opening
**Next row (WS)** Continuing in B, p10, bind off next 15 sts, p to end. **Next row** K8, cast on 15, k to end. Continuing in B work one repeat of Tuck pat. Change color. Work 13 more repeats of Tuck Pat in following color sequence: A, C, A, B, A, C, A, B, A, C, A, B, A. Bind off.

## FINISHING
Sew ends of fabric together leaving a 3"/7.5cm opening for spout. Using doubled yarn and tapestry needle, gather the top by piercing through the top end of each welt and pull gently. Secure in place with needle and thread, making sure the welts are layered and angled nicely. Make one 4"/10cm pompom using all three colors and sew to top.

# HEAD IN THE Clouds

Rose Callahan

## YOU'LL NEED:

### YARN ④
*Superwash Merino Cashmere* by Lion Brand Co. 1½oz/40g, 87yd/80m merino wool, nylon and cashmere blend in light sky blue (MC) and ivory (CC)

### NEEDLES
One pair size 7 (4.5mm) knitting needles or *size to obtain gauge*

### ADDITIONAL MATERIALS
Crochet hook size H/8 (5mm)
Stitch holder
Yarn needle
½ yd fleece fabric
Sewing thread
Buckwheat hulls or fiberfill stuffing
3½" (13mm) pearl buttons

## SIZE
One size.

## MEASUREMENTS
**Width** 13"/33 cm
**Length** 12"/30.5 cm

## GAUGES
17 sts and 25 rows to 4"/10 cm over St st using size 8 (5 mm) needles.
*Take time to check gauge.*

**Note** Clouds are embroidered in duplicate st after front piece has been knitted. When referring to "right" front or "left" front, we're talking about the neck pillow as it is worn.

## PILLOW
### Right front
With MC, cast on 7 sts. **Rows 1, 3, 5 (RS)** Inc, k to last st, inc. **Rows 2 and 4** Inc, p to last st, inc. **Row 6** Purl. Rep rows 5-6 three times more—23 sts. Work 12 rows even in St st. **Row 25 (RS)** Inc, k across. Work 3 rows even in St st. **Row 29 (RS)** Rep row 25. **Row 30** Purl. **Row 31** Rep row 25. **Row 32** Purl across to last st, inc—27 sts. Place all sts on holder.

### Left front
Work as for rows 1-32 of right front, reversing all shaping, do not put sts on holder.
**Row 33 (RS)** Knit to end, cast on 4 sts, k across 27 sts on holder—58 sts. Work 19 rows even in St st. **Row 53 (RS)** Ssk, k to last 2 sts, k2tog—56 sts. Work 3 rows even in St st. **Row 57 (RS)** Rep row 53—54 sts. Work 1 row even in St st. Rep last 2 rows 4 times more—46 sts. **Row 67** Rep row 53—44 sts. **Row 68** P2tog, p across, ssp—42 sts. Rep last 2 rows once more—38 sts. Bind off 4 sts at beg of next 2 rows, 6 sts at beg of next 2 rows. Bind off rem 18 sts.

### Bottom back
**Note** Back is made in 2 pieces.
With CC, work as for front through row 52.
**Rows 53-56** Work in k1, p1 rib. Bind off.
### Top back
With CC, cast on 58 sts. **Rows 1-4** Work in k1, p1 rib. **Row 5 (buttonhole row)** [K13, k2tog, yo] 3 times, k13. **Row 6** Purl. Complete to match front, starting with row 53.

## FINISHING
Steam all pieces. Using CC and yarn needle, follow chart to embroider clouds in duplicate stitch, spacing them randomly over front (sample shows 7 clouds, 3 of which are reversed image of chart). Trace around front to make a liner pattern. Cut out 2 identical liner pieces from fleece fabric and sew tog leaving a gap for stuffing. Clip seams and turn right side out, stuffing with buckwheat hulls or fiberfill. Sew gap. Pin knitted back pieces to front, overlapping ribbed edge of top back over ribbed edge of lower back. With MC, crochet hook and front facing, work a rnd of sc around entire edge, followed by 2 rnds of sl st. Fasten off. Sew buttons on ribbed edge of bottom back. Place stuffed pillow inside cover.

color key
■ light blue
□ cream
10 sts

# HEAD Scarf

Marcus Tullis

## YOU'LL NEED:

### YARN (4)
3oz/85g, 200yd/190m of any worsted weight chenille yarn

### NEEDLES
One size 7 (4.5mm) circular needle, 29"/74cm long or *size to obtain gauge*
Two size 7 (4.5mm) double-pointed needles (dpns) for ties

## SIZE
One size. Sized for adult woman.

## MEASUREMENTS
Approximately 18"/45.5cm wide x 13"/33cm at longest point (without ties)

## GAUGE
20 sts and 28 rows to 4"/10cm over St st using size 7 (4.5mm) needles.
*Take time to check gauge.*

**Note** A circular needle is used to accommodate the large number of sts. Work back and forth in rows.

## HEAD SCARF
Cast on 91 sts.
**Rolled edge**
Purl 1 row on RS, knit 1 row on WS.
**Row 1 (RS)** SSK, k to last 2 sts, k2tog.
**Row 2** Purl.
Rep rows 1 and 2 until 3 sts rem, ending with a WS row.
**Next row** Sl 1, k2tog, psso. Fasten off.

## TIES (make 2)
With dpn, cast on 4 sts. Work I-cord as foll:
**\*Next row (RS)** K4. Slide sts back to beg of needle so that next row is a RS row; rep from * until tie measures 10"/25.5cm long. Bind off.

## FINISHING
Sew ends of ties to long edge of scarf, letting edge roll around ties.

# LACE Snood

Rose Callahan

## YOU'LL NEED:

### YARN
10½oz/300g, 330yd/310m of any bulky weight cotton yarn

### NEEDLES
One size 10 (6mm) circular needle 24"/60cm long or *size to obtain gauge*

### ADDITIONAL MATERIALS
Stitch marker

### SIZE
One size. Sized for adult woman.

### MEASUREMENTS
**Circumference** Approximately 38"/96.5cm
**Width** 15"/38cm

### GAUGE
13½ sts and 21 rows to 4"/10cm over lace chart, using size 10 (6mm) needles.
*Take time to check gauge.*

### STITCH GLOSSARY
**Seed stitch** (over an even number of sts)
**Rnd 1** *K1, p1; rep from * around.
**Rnd 2** P the knit sts, and k the purl sts.
Rep rnd 2 for seed st.

### SNOOD
Cast on 130 sts, pm for beg of rnd and join, being careful not to twist sts on needle. Work 4 rnds in seed st.
**Beg chart pattern**
Work the 10-st rep of lace chart 13 times around.
When the 12 rnds of the lace chart have been worked 5 times, work rnds 1-6 once more. Work 4 rnds seed st. Bind off.

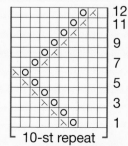

**STITCH KEY**
☐ k on RS
⊙ yo
⊠ k2tog
⊠ ssk

10-st repeat

# MOBIUS Cowl

Rose Callahan

## YOU'LL NEED:

### YARN
3½oz/100g, 340yd/310m of any
worsted weight wool blend yarn

### NEEDLES
One size 5 (3.75mm) circular needle,
24"/60cm long or *size to obtain gauge*

### SIZE
One size. Sized for adult woman.

### MEASUREMENTS
**Circumference** 30"/76cm
**Width** 9"/23cm

### GAUGE
24 sts and 32 rnds to 4"/10cm over pattern
stitch, using size 5 (3.75mm) needles.
*Take time to check gauge.*

### STITCH GLOSSARY
**Pattern stitch** (multiple of 12 sts)
**Rnds 1 and 2** Knit.
**Rnds 3 and 4** K3, *p7, k5; rep from * to last 9
sts, p7, k2.
**Rnds 5-8** Rep rnds 1-4.
**Rnds 9 and 10** Knit.
**Rnds 11 and 12** P4, *k5, p7; rep from * to last
8 sts, k5, p3.
**Rnds 13-16** Rep rnds 9-12.
Rep rnds 1-16 for pattern stitch.

### COWL
Cast on 180 sts, twist sts once on needle,
pm and join for knitting in the round.
(**Note** To twist, before joining be sure that
all sts are facing the same way, then take
last group of sts cast-on and twist them
360 degrees around needle. Join and work
around as usual.)
Work in pattern stitch until piece measures
approx 9"/23cm or desired length from beg,
end with row 8 or 16.
Bind off.

# BOOT Toppers

Paul Amato for ivarepresents.com

## YOU'LL NEED:

### YARN
3½oz/100g, 190yd/170m of any worsted weight wool yarn

### NEEDLES
Size 8 (5mm) circular needle 12"/30cm long, or *size to obtain gauge*

### ADDITIONAL MATERIALS
Stitch markers

## SIZE
One size. Sized for adult woman.

## MEASUREMENTS
**Width over faux cable section**
15½"/39.5cm
**Length** 8"/20.5cm

## GAUGE
18 sts and 22 rnds to 4"/10cm over faux cable/rib pat using size 8 (5mm) needles.
*Take time to check gauge.*

## STITCH GLOSSARY
**Faux cable/rib pat**
(multiple of 5 sts)
**Rnds 1 and 2** *P1, k3, p1; rep from * around. **Rnd 3** *P1, sl 1 purlwise wyib, k2, pass the slipped st over the k2, p1; rep from * around. **Rnd 4** *P1, k1, yo, k1, p1; rep from * around. Rep rnds 1-4 for faux cable/rib pat. **Note** Pat begins and ends with a p1 for a neater join at the beg of rounds.

## TOPPER (make 2)
Cast on 70 sts. Join, taking care not to twist sts. Place marker for beg of rnd and sl marker every rnd. Work in faux cable/rib pat for 20 rnds. Cont in rib only (rep rnd 1) until piece measures 8"/20.5cm from beg. Bind off in rib.

## YOU'LL NEED:

### YARN

**Tablet case**
4oz/120g, 190yd/180m of any worsted weight wool blend yarn in brown (MC) and yellow (CC)

**Phone case**
Small amounts of any worsted weight wool blend yarn in white (MC) and brown (CC)

### NEEDLES
One set (5) size 6 (4mm) double-pointed needles (dpns) *or size to obtain gauge*

### ADDITIONAL MATERIALS
One button
Stitch markers

## SIZES
Shown in sizes 1 (tablet) with changes for 7 (phone) in parentheses.

## MEASUREMENTS
**Tablet (Phone)**
**Height** 9½ (4½)"/24 (11.5)cm
**Width** 7½ (2½)"/19 (6.5)cm
**Depth** ½"/1.5cm

## GAUGE
24 sts and 30 rows to 4"/10cm over St st using size 6 (4mm) needles.
*Take time to check gauge.*

## COVER
With MC, cast on 96 (36) of sts. Distribute over 4 dpn, join being careful not to twist sts, and pm for beg of rnd.

**Beg chart**
Working only between lines for desired size, work rnd 1 of chart twice (for each side of cover). Cont to work chart in this manner through rnd 12. Rep rnds 1-12 until piece measures ½"/1.5cm

longer than device.

## BRAID TRIM
**Rnd 1** *K1 MC, k1 CC; rep from * around. Bring both colors to front.
**Rnd 2** *P1 MC, p1 CC, always bringing new color over last color; rep from * around.
**Rnd 3** *P1 MC, p1 CC, always bringing new color under last color; rep from * around.
Bind off with CC.

## FINISHING
Sew bound-off edge to inside of braid.
**I-cord loop**
With dpn and color of choice, cast on 3 (2) sts.
***Next row (RS)** K3 (2). Do not turn. Slide sts to beg of needle to work next row from RS. Rep from * for approx 4"/10cm or desired length. K3tog and fasten off last st. Attach

I-cord to center edge of back opening. Insert device in cover to determine button placement on front. Sew on button.

### STITCH AND COLOR KEY
☐ k     ☑ slip 1 wyib     ■ MC     ☐ CC

size 8 (16-st side)
size 7 (18-st side)
size 6 (20-st side)
size 5 (28-st side)
size 4 (32-st side)
size 3 (34-st side)
size 2 (46-st side)
size 1 (48-st side)

12
10
1
set-up rnd

# BUTTON NECK Scarf

## YOU'LL NEED:

### YARN
3½oz/100g, 110yd/100m of any
worsted weight wool yarn

### NEEDLES
One pair size 6 (4mm) knitting needles
or *size to obtain gauge*

### ADDITIONAL MATERIALS
Three 1½"/4cm buttons
Sewing needle and matching thread

## SIZE
One size. Sized for adult woman.

## MEASUREMENTS
Approximately 5½" x 26"/14cm x 66cm

## GAUGE
32 sts and 26 rows to 4"/10cm over k3,
p2 rib (unstretched) using size 6 (4mm)
needles.
*Take time to check gauge.*

## STITCH GLOSSARY
**K3, p2 rib** (multiple of 5 sts plus 3)
**Row 1 (RS)** *K3, p2; rep from * to last 3 sts,
k3. **Row 2 (WS)** *P3, k2; rep from * to last 3
sts, p3. Rep rows 1 and 2 for k3, p2 rib.

## SCARF
Cast on 48 sts. Work in k3, p2 rib for
25½"/64.5cm, end with a RS row.
**Next (buttonhole) row (WS)** P3, k2tog, yo,
[p3, k2] 3 times, p3, k2tog, yo, [p3, k2] 3
times, p3, yo, k2tog, p3. Work 3 rows in k3,
p2 rib. Bind off loosely in rib.

## FINISHING
Sew buttons to right side of scarf at
15"/38cm, 16½"/42cm, 18"/45.5cm from
buttonhole edge.

Rose Callahan

# TEXTURED Cowl

Rose Callahan

## YOU'LL NEED:

### YARN
3½oz/100g, 120yd/110m of any DK weight wool yarn

### NEEDLES
One size 8 (5mm) circular needle, 24"/60cm long, or *size to obtain gauge*

### ADDITIONAL MATERIALS
Stitch markers

## SIZE
One size. Sized for adult woman.

## MEASUREMENTS
**Circumference** Approx 31½"/80cm
**Length** 8"/20.5cm

## GAUGE
18 sts and 30 rnds to 4"/10cm over pattern st using size 8 (5mm) needle. *Take time to check gauge.*

## STITCH GLOSSARY
**Pattern stitch** (multiple of 6 sts plus 5)
**Rnd 1** K2, *p3, k3; rep from * end p3.
**Rnd 2** *K1, p1; rep from * to last st, k1.
Rep rnds 1 and 2 for pattern stitch.

## COWL
Cast on 149 sts, twist sts once on needle, pm and join for knitting in the round. (**Note** To twist, before joining be sure that all sts are facing the same way, then take last group of sts cast-on and twist them 360 degrees around needle. Join, pm and work around as usual.)

**Beg pattern stitch**
Work in pattern stitch until piece measures 8"/20.5cm from beg. Bind off.

Rose Callahan

## YOU'LL NEED:

### YARN 4
3½oz/100g, 420yd/390m of any worsted weight wool yarn

### NEEDLES
One pair size 10 (6mm) needles or *size to obtain gauge*

### ADDITIONAL MATERIALS
Cable needle (cn)
Ten ½"/12mm buttons

### SIZE
One size. Sized for adult woman.

### MEASUREMENTS
**Circumference (buttoned)** 7½"/19cm
**Length (wrist to fingers)** 7"/18cm

### GAUGE
20 sts and 35 rows to 4"/10cm over St st using size 10 (6mm) needles.
*Take time to check gauge.*

## STITCH GLOSSARY
**4-st RC** Sl 2 sts to cn and hold to *back*, k2, k2 from cn.
**4-st LC** Sl 2 sts to cn and hold to *front*, k2, k2 from cn.

## LEFT HAND WARMER
With size 10 (6mm) needles, cast on 35 sts. Knit 2 rows. **Next (buttonhole) row (WS)** K3, [yo, k2tog, k5] 4 times, yo, k2tog, k2. Knit 2 rows.
**Beg back of hand**
**Row 1 (RS)** K10 for wristband, p2, [k4, p2] 3 times, k5. **Rows 2 and 4** K7, [p4, k2] 3 times, k10. **Row 3** K10, p2 [4-st RC, p2] 3 times, k5. **Rows 5 and 6** Rep rows 1 and 2. Rep rows 1–6 4 times more, then rep rows 1–5 once more. Knit 1 row.
**Thumb opening**
**Next row (RS)** K12, bind off 10 sts, k to end. **Next row** K13, cast on 10 sts over bound-off sts, k to end.
**Palm**
Work in garter st (k every row) until piece measures 3½"/9cm from thumb opening. Bind off.

## RIGHT HAND WARMER
Cast on and work as for Left Hand Warmer, end with buttonhole row.
**Beg back of hand**
**Row 1 (RS)** K5, p2, [k4, p2] 3 times, k10 for wristband. **Rows 2 and 4** K12, [p4, k2] 3 times, k5. **Row 3** K5, p2 [4-st LC, p2] 3 times, k10. **Rows 5 and 6** Rep rows 1 and 2. Rep rows 1–6 4 times more, then rep rows 1–5 once more. Knit 1 row.
**Thumb opening**
**Next row (RS)** K13, bind off 10 sts, k to end of row. **Next row** K12, cast on 10 sts over bound-off sts, k to end.
**Palm**
Work as for Left Hand Warmer.

## FINISHING
Sew on buttons opposite buttonholes.

# HIS AND HER Hats

Jack Deutsch

## YOU'LL NEED:

### YARN ⑤
**Woman's hat**
1¾oz/50g, 140yd/130m (1¾oz/50g, 140yd/130m; 3½oz/100g, 210yd/190m) of any bulky weight wool yarn in pink (MC)
⅞ oz/25g in pastel yellow (A) and gold (B)

**Man's hat**
1¾oz/50g, 140yd/130m (1¾oz/50g, 140yd/130m; 3½oz/100g, 210yd/190m) of any bulky weight wool yarn in light blue (MC)
⅞oz/25g in yellow (A) and navy (B)

### NEEDLES
Size 8 (5mm) circular knitting needle, 16"/41cm long or *size to obtain gauge*
One set (4) size 8 (5mm) double-pointed needles (dpns)

### ADDITIONAL MATERIALS
Stitch marker
Tapestry needle

▮▮▮▯▯

## SIZES
Instructions are written for adult size Small. Changes for Medium and Large are in parentheses.

## MEASUREMENTS
**Circumference** 19 (21, 23)"/48.5 (53.5, 58.5)cm
**Height** 7½ (8, 8½)"/19 (20.5, 21.5)cm

## GAUGE
22 sts and 22 rows to 4"/10cm over rib pattern using size 8 (5mm) needles.
*Take time to check gauge.*

## STITCH GLOSSARY
**Rib pattern** (multiple of 11 sts)
**Rnd 1** *K4, [p1, k1] 3 times, p1; rep from * around.
Rep rnd 1 for rib pattern.

## HAT
With MC cast on 88 (99, 110) sts. Join to work in rnds, taking care not to twist sts. Place marker for beg of rnds.
**Next rnd** Work 11-st rep of rib pat 8 (9, 10) times around.
Work in rib pat for 7 rnds more.
With A work 4 rnds rib pat.
With MC work 2 rnds rib pat.

With B work 2 rnds rib pat.
With MC work even until hat measures 6 (6½, 7)"/15 (16.5, 18)cm.

## SHAPE CROWN
**Next (dec) rnd** *K4, p1, ssk, k1, k2tog, p1; rep from * around—72 (81, 90) sts. **Next rnd** *K4, p1, k3, p1; rep from * around. Work even for 3 rnds. **Next (dec) rnd** *Ssk, k2tog, p1, k3, p1; rep from * around—56 (63, 70) sts. **Next rnd** *K2, p1, k3, p1; rep from * around. Work even for 3 rnds. **Next (dec) rnd** *K2, p1, S2KP, p1; rep from * around—40 (45, 50) sts. **Next rnd** *K2, p1, k1, p1; rep from * around. **Next (dec) rnd** *K2tog, k1, ssk; rep from * around—24 (27, 30) sts.
Work 1 rnd even.

## FINISHING
With yarn needle, pull yarn through rem sts several times, closing hole at top.

# RUFFLED Cuffs

Paul Amato for lvarepresents.com

## YOU'LL NEED:

### YARN ③
1¾oz/50g, 160yd/140m of any DK weight wool blend yarn

### NEEDLES
One set (5) size 5 (3.75mm) dpns or *size to obtain gauge*

## SIZE
One size. Sized for adult woman.

## MEASUREMENTS
**Circumference** Approx 6"/15cm, (will stretch to fit up to 9"/23cm)
**Length** 6"/15cm

## GAUGE
26 sts and 34 rows to 4"/10cm over lace chart using size 5 (3.75mm) needles.
*Take time to check gauge.*

## CUFF (make 2)
### Ruffle
With dpns, cast on 80 sts. Divide sts evenly over 4 dpns (20 sts on dpn). Place marker (pm) and join, being careful not to twist sts. P 1 rnd, k 4 rnds. **Next rnd** *K2tog; rep from * around—40 sts.
### Beg chart
**Rnd 1** Work 20-st rep chart 2 times around. When 28 rnds of chart pat are complete, work rnds 1–14 once more. Work in k1, p1 rib for 4 rnds. Bind off loosely.

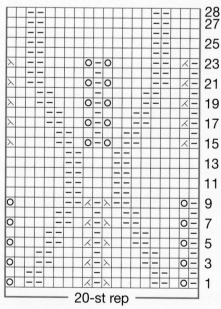

Chart row numbers (right side): 1, 3, 5, 7, 9, 11, 13, 15, 17, 19, 21, 23, 25, 27, 28

**20-st rep**

## STITCH KEY
☐ k on RS     ⊡ yo
⊟ p on RS     ⊠ k2tog
                     ⊠ ssk

# FINGERLESS Mitts

## YOU'LL NEED:

### YARN
4oz/120g, 190yd/180m of any worsted weight wool blend yarn

### NEEDLES
One set (5) size 4 (3.5mm) double-pointed needles (dpns) or *size to obtain gauge*

### ADDITIONAL MATERIALS
Stitch markers
Scrap yarn

## SIZE
One size. Sized for adult woman.

## MEASUREMENTS
**Wrist circumference** 8"/20.5cm
**Length** 9"/23cm

## GAUGE
20 sts and 32 rnds to 4"/10cm over St st using size 4 (3.5mm) needles.
*Take time to check gauge.*

## STITCH GLOSSARY
**Double broken rib** (multiple of 4 sts)
**Rnds 1 and 2** *K2, p2; rep from * around.
**Rnd 3** Knit.
**Rnd 4** Purl.
Rep rnds 1–4 for double broken rib.
**Offset broken rib** (multiple of 4 sts)
**Rnds 1 and 2** K1, *p2, k2; rep from * to last 3 sts, p2, k1.
**Rnd 3** Knit.
**Rnd 4** Purl.
**Rnds 5 and 6** P1, *k2, p2; rep from * to last 3 sts, k2, p1.
**Rnd 7** Knit.
**Rnd 8** Purl.
Rep rnds 1–8 for offset broken rib.

## RIGHT MITT
Cast on 40 sts and divide evenly over 4 dpn (10 sts on each needle). Join, taking care not to twist sts, and place marker (pm) for beg of rnd.
Work in double broken rib until piece measures 4"/10cm from beg, end with a rnd 4.
**Hand**
**Next rnd** K9, work rnd 1 of offset broken rib over next 20 sts, k to end of rnd.
Cont in this manner until 8 rnds of offset rib pat are complete.
**Thumb gusset**
**Next (inc) rnd** Cont in pat as established to last 10 sts, pm, M1, k1, M1, pm, k to end of rnd—42 sts.
Work one rnd even.
**Next (inc) rnd** Work to first gusset marker, sl marker, M1, knit to next marker, M1, sl marker, work to end of rnd—44 sts.
Rep inc rnd every other rnd 5 times more—15 sts between gusset markers.
**Next rnd** Work to first gusset marker, place next 15 sts on scrap yarn for thumb, cast

on 3 sts, work to end of rnd—42 sts.
Work even until piece measures 9"/23cm from beg, end with a row 3 or 7. Bind off purlwise.
**Thumb**
Place the 15 thumb sts on 2 dpns. Rejoin yarn and with 3rd dpn, pick up and k 5 sts along thumb opening, k15. Pm for beg of rnd. Work 3 rnds in St st (k every rnd).
**Next (dec) rnd** Ssk, k1, k2tog, k to end of rnd—18 sts. Work 5 rnds even. Bind off purlwise.

## LEFT MITT
Work same as for right mitt to thumb gusset.
**Thumb gusset**
K7, pm, M1, k1, M1, pm, cont in pat as established. Complete as for right mitt.

# SELF-STRIPING Gauntlets

## YOU'LL NEED:

### YARN (4)
5¼oz/150g, 100yd/90m of any worsted weight self-striping wool blend yarn

### NEEDLES
One set (4) size 4 (3.5mm) dpns or *size to obtain gauge*

### ADDITIONAL MATERIALS
Cable needle (cn)
Stitch holders

## SIZE
One size. Sized for adult woman.

## MEASUREMENTS
**Hand circumference** 8"/20.5cm

## GAUGE
24 sts and 28 rnds to 4"/10cm over cable pat using size 4 (3.5mm) dpn.
*Take time to check gauge.*

## STITCH GLOSSARY
**K2, p1 rib** (multiple of 4 sts)
**Rnd 1 (RS)** *K2, p2; rep from * around.
Rep this rnd for k2, p2 rib.
**Cable pattern** (multiple of 8 sts)
**Rnds 1–3 (RS)** *K4, p4; rep from * around.
**Rnd 4** *Sl next 2 sts to cn and hold in *front*, k2, k2 from cn, p4; rep from * around.
**Rnds 5 and 6** Rep rnd 1.
Rep rnds 1–6 for cable pat.

## GAUNTLET (make 2)
Cast on 48 sts dividing sts evenly between 3 dpns. Join taking care not to twist sts on dpns. Place marker for end of rnd and sl marker every rnd. Work in cable pat until piece measures 6"/15cm from beg.

### Thumb gusset
**Inc rnd 1** Work cable pat across first 4 sts, pm, [M1] twice, pm, work cable pat to end—50 sts. Work next rnd even, working sts between thumb gusset markers in St st.
**Inc rnd 2** Work cable pat across first 4 sts, sl marker, M1, k2, M1, sl marker, work cable pat to end—52 sts. Work next rnd even.
**Inc rnd 3** Work cable pat across first 4 sts, sl marker, M1, k4, M1, sl marker, work cable pat to end—54 sts. Work next rnd even.
**Inc rnd 4** Work cable pat across first 4 sts, sl marker, M1, k6, M1, sl marker, work cable pat to end—56 sts. Work next rnd even.
**Inc rnd 5** Work cable pat across first 4 sts, sl marker, M1, k8, M1, sl marker, work cable pat to end—58 sts. Work next rnd even.
**Inc rnd 6** Work cable pat across first 4 sts, sl marker, M1, k10, M1, sl marker, work cable pat to end—60 sts. Work next rnd even.
**Inc rnd 7** Work cable pat across first 4 sts, sl marker, M1, k12, M1, sl marker, work cable pat to end—62 sts. Work next rnd even.

**Inc rnd 8** Work cable pat across first 4 sts, sl marker, M1, k14, M1, sl marker, work cable pat to end—64 sts. Work next 3 rnds even.
**Next rnd** Work cable pat across first 4 sts, place next 16 sts on two separate holders (8 sts on each) for thumb, work cable pat to end—48 sts. Cont in cable pat until piece measures 12"/30.5cm from beg, end on rnd 6. Bind off in cable pat.

### Thumb
Place 16 sts on holders to 3 dpn, dividing sts evenly. Join and place marker for end of rnd and sl marker every rnd. Work in St st for 4 rnds. Cont in k2, p2 rib for 5 rnds. Bind off in rib.

Jack Deutsch

# BOBBLE Cowl

## YOU'LL NEED:

### YARN (5)
3½oz/100g, 240yd/220m of any bulky weight wool blend yarn

### NEEDLES
One pair size 10 (6mm) needles or *size to obtain gauge*

### ADDITIONAL MATERIALS
Small amount of scrap yarn
Size J/10 (6mm) crochet hook (for provisional cast-on)

## SIZE
One size. Sized for adult woman.

## MEASUREMENTS
**Circumference** 21½"/54.5cm
**Depth** 9"/23cm

## GAUGE
16 sts and 26 rows to 4"/10cm over garter st using size 10 (6mm) needles.
*Take time to check gauge.*

## STITCH GLOSSARY
**Pattern stitch**
**Rows 1-4** Slip 1, k to end. **Row 5** Knit on 2 sts, [k1, p1, k1, p1, k1] into first st, [turn, k5] 5 times, turn, slip 2nd, 3rd, 4th and 5th sts one at a time over first st, working first st, k1 tbl, bind off 2 sts, k to end.

## SPECIAL TECHNIQUES
**Knit on 2 sts** At the beg of the row, *k1 without dropping the stitch from the LH needle, place new stitch on LH needle; rep from * in new stitch.
**Provisional cast-on**
Using scrap yarn and crochet hook, chain the number of sts to cast on, plus a few extra. Cut a tail and pull the tail through the last chain. With knitting needle and yarn, pick up and knit the stated number of sts through the "bumps" on the back of the chain. To remove scrap chain, when instructed, pull out the tail from the last crochet st. Gently and slowly pull on the tail to unravel the crochet sts, carefully placing each released knit st on a needle.

## 3-Needle Bind-Off
**1** Hold right sides of pieces together on two needles. Insert third needle knitwise into first st of each needle, and wrap yarn knitwise.
**2** Knit these two sts together, and slip them off the needles. *Knit the next two sts together in the same manner.
**3** Slip first st on 3rd needle over 2nd st and off needle. Rep from * in step 2 across row until all sts are bound off.

## Notes
**1** The provisional cast-on is optional. To eliminate it, cast on as usual and bind off when knitting is complete. Then seam the 2 ends tog.
**2** The stitch pattern is a 5-row repeat. This results in bobbles being worked on alternating side edges.

## COWL
Using provisional cast on, cast on 36 sts. Work in pattern stitch until 5-row rep has been worked 28 times. Piece measures approx 21½"/54.5cm from beg.

## FINISHING
Carefully unravel scrap yarn chain and place live sts onto second needle. Graft ends tog or join using 3-needle bind-off. To wear, fold upper edge to RS as in photo.

Paul Amato for lvarepresents.com

## YOU'LL NEED:

### YARN (3)
3½oz/100g, 230yd/210m of any DK weight wool yarn

### NEEDLES
One set (4) size 5 (3.75mm) double-pointed needles *or size to obtain gauge*

### ADDITIONAL MATERIALS
Scrap yarn

### SIZE
One size. Sized for adult man.

### MEASUREMENTS
**Hand circumference** 7"/18cm
**Length** 8"/20.5cm

### GAUGE
26 sts and 28 rnds to 4"/10cm over twisted rib pat using size 5 (3.75mm) dpns.
*Take time to check gauge*

### STITCH GLOSSARY
**Cuff Rib** (multiple of 5 sts)
**Rnd 1** *K3, p2; rep from * around.
Rep rnd 1 for cuff rib.

**Twisted Rib** (multiple of 5 sts)
**Rnd 1** *P3, k2 tbl; rep from * around.
Rep rnd 1 for twisted rib.

### MITT (make 2)
Cast on 45 sts. Join, being careful not to twist sts, and pm for beg of rnd. Work in cuff rib until piece measures 2"/5cm from beg. Change to twisted rib and work until piece measures 4½"/11.5cm from beg.
**Thumb opening**
**Next rnd** Work 10 sts in twisted rib, place next 8 sts on scrap yarn, cast on 8 sts, cont in twisted rib to end of rnd. Cont in twisted rib over all sts until piece measures 7"/18cm from beg. Work in cuff rib for 1"/2.5cm. Bind off in pat.

### THUMB
Place sts from scrap yarn to dpn. Rejoin yarn and work in twisted rib as established over 8 sts. With free dpn, pick up and k 2 sts tbl along side edge of thumb opening, pick up and rib 8 sts in the cast-on sts above thumb opening, pick up and k 2 sts tbl along side edge of opening. Divide sts on 3 dpns. Work in twisted rib as established for 1¾"/4.5cm. Bind off knitwise.

Paul Amato for livarepresents.com

## YOU'LL NEED:

### YARN ⬤3
1¾oz/50g, 120yd/110m of any DK weight wool yarn

### NEEDLES
One set (4) size 5 (3.75mm) double-pointed needles *or size to obtain gauge*

### ADDITIONAL MATERIALS
Scrap yarn

### SIZES
One size. Sized for adult woman.

### MEASUREMENTS
**Hand circumference** 6"/16.5cm
**Length** 7"/18cm

### GAUGE
26 sts and 28 rnds to 4"/10cm over twisted rib pat using size 5 (3.75mm) dpns.
*Take time to check gauge*

### STITCH GLOSSARY
**Cuff Rib** (multiple of 3 sts)
**Rnd 1** *K2, p1; rep from * around.
Rep rnd 1 for cuff rib.
**Twisted Rib** (multiple of 3 sts)
**Rnd 1** *P2, k1 tbl; rep from * around.
Rep rnd 1 for twisted rib.

### MITT (make 2)
Cast on 39 sts. Join, being careful not to twist sts, and pm for beg of rnd. Work in cuff rib until piece measures 2"/5cm from beg. Change to twisted rib and work until piece measures 4"/10cm from beg.

### Thumb opening
**Next rnd** Work 9 sts in twisted rib, place next 5 sts on scrap yarn, cast on 5 sts, cont in twisted rib to end of rnd. Cont in twisted rib over all sts until piece measures 6"/15cm from beg. Work in cuff rib for 1"/2.5cm. Bind off in pat.

### THUMB
Place sts from scrap yarn to dpn. Rejoin yarn and work in twisted rib as established over 5 sts. with free dpn, pick up and k 1 st tbl along the side of thumb opening, pick up and rib 5 sts in the cast-on sts above thumb opening, pick up and k 1 st tbl along side edge of opening. Divide sts on 3 dpns. Work in twisted rib as established for 1¾"/4.5cm. Bind off knitwise.

Paul Amato for lvarepresents.com

## YOU'LL NEED:

### YARN
7oz/200g, 370yd/340m of any
worsted weight wool blend yarn

### NEEDLES
One pair size 9 (5.5mm) needles *or
size to obtain gauge*

### ADDITIONAL MATERIALS
Cable needle (cn)

## SIZE
One size. Sized for adult woman.

## MEASUREMENTS
**Circumference** 28"/71cm
**Length** 9½"/24cm

## GAUGE
26 sts and 24 rows to 4"/10cm over reversible cable pat using size 9 (5.5mm) needles.
*Take time to check gauge.*

## STITCH GLOSSARY
**12-st RC** Sl 6 sts to cn and hold to *back*, [k1, p1] 3 times, [k1, p1] 3 times from cn.
**Reversible cable pattern**
(multiple of 17 sts, plus 12)
**Row 1-6** *[K1, p1] 6 times, k5; rep from * to last 12 sts, [k1, p1] 6 times.
**Row 7** *12-st RC, k5; rep from * to last 12 sts, 12-st RC.
**Rows 8–13** Rep rows 1-6.
Rep rows 1–13 for cable pattern.

## COWL
Cast on 63 sts. Work in reversible cable pat for 28"/71cm, ending with a row 6 or 13. Bind off. Sew cast-on and bound-off edges tog.

Paul Amato for lvarepresents.com

# MOUNTAIN Mitts

Jack Deutsch

## YOU'LL NEED:

### YARN
3½oz/100g, 110yd/100m of any bulky weight wool yarn each in burgundy (A), orange (B), green (C), black (D), red (E), light blue (F), violet (G), and dark purple (H)

### NEEDLES
One set (4) size 8 (5mm) double-pointed needles (dpns) or *size to obtain gauge*
One set (4) size 7 (4.5mm) double-pointed needles (dpns)

### ADDITIONAL MATERIALS
Stitch markers
Yarn needle

## SIZE
One size. Sized for adult woman.

## MEASUREMENTS
**Circumference** 8"/20cm

## GAUGE
18 sts and 24 rnds to 4"/10cm over Slip st pat using larger dpns.
*Take time to check gauge.*

## STITCH GLOSSARY
**M1L (make 1 left)** Lift the bar between stitches so that the yarn goes from front to back over the needle. Knit into the back of this stitch so that it makes a loop when removed from the needle.

**M1R (make 1 right)** Lift the bar between stitches so that the yarn goes from back to front over the needle. Knit into the front of this stitch so that it makes a loop when removed from the needle.

**K1, p1 rib**
(worked over an even number of sts)
**Row 1** *K1, p1; rep from * to end.
Repeat row 1 for k1, p1 rib.

**Slip st pattern**
(worked over a multiple of 18 sts)
**Rnd 1 (RS)** With B [k5, sl 1] 3 times.
**Rnd 2** With B knit. **Rnd 3** With C k2, [sl 1, k5] twice, sl 1, k3. **Rnd 4** With C knit. Rep rnds 1–4 for Slip st pat, following color sequence.

## GLOVE (make 2)
### Cuff
With smaller dpns and A, cast on 34 sts. Divide evenly over three needles being careful not to twist sts. Join and place marker for end of rnd, sl marker every rnd. Work in k1, p1 rib until piece measures 2½"/7cm. **Next rnd** With larger dpns, knit, inc 3 sts evenly spaced––37 sts.

### Hand and thumb
**Note** The hand is worked in Slip st pat, the thumb in St st. Slip markers every rnd.
**Rnd 1 (RS)** With B [k5, sl 1] 3 times, place thumb marker, M1L, k1, M1R, place thumb marker, [k5, sl 1] 3 times—39 sts. **Rnd 2** With B knit. **Rnd 3** With C k2, [sl 1, k5] twice, sl 1, k3, k3 for thumb, k2, [sl 1, k5] twice, sl 1, k3. **Rnd 4** With C k18, M1L, k3, M1R, k18—41 sts. **Rnd 5** With D [k5, sl 1] 3 times, k5 for thumb, [k5, sl 1] 3 times.
**Rnd 6** With D knit. **Rnd 7** With E k2, [sl 1, k5] twice, sl 1, k3, M1L, k5, M1R, k2, [sl 1, k5] twice, sl 1, k3—43 sts. **Rnd 8** With E knit.
**Rnd 9** With F [k5, sl 1] 3 times, k7 for thumb, [k5, sl 1] 3 times. **Rnd 10** With F k18, M1L, k7, M1R, k18—45 sts. **Rnd 11** With G k2, [sl 1, k5] twice, sl 1, k3, k9 for thumb, k2, [sl 1, k5] twice, sl 1, k3. **Rnd 12** With G knit.
**Rnd 13** With H [k5, sl 1] 3 times, M1L, k9, M1R, [k5, sl 1] 3 times—47 sts. **Rnd 14** With H knit. **Rnd 15** With A k2, [sl 1, k5] twice, sl 1, k2, remove thumb marker, place 11 thumb sts on holder, cast on 2 sts, k3, [sl 1, k5] twice, sl 1, k3—38 sts. **Rnd 16** With A k17, SKP, k2tog, k17—36 sts. **Rnd 17** With B [k5, sl 1] 6 times. **Rnd 18** With B knit.
**Rnd 19** With C k2, sl 1, [k5, sl 1] 5 times, k3. **Rnd 20** With C knit. **Rnd 21** With D [k5, sl 1] 6 times. **Rnd 22** With D knit. **Rnd 23** With E k2, sl 1, [k5, sl 1] 5 times, k3. **Rnd 24** With E knit.

### Little finger
**Next rnd** With E k4, slip next 28 sts to holder, cast on 1 st, k last 4 sts—9 sts. Knit 5 rnds. Bind off purlwise. Slip 28 sts back to larger dpns. **Next rnd** With E knit 28, pick up and knit 1 st in little finger's cast-on st—29 sts. Knit 1 row.

### Ring finger
**Next rnd** With F k5, slip next 19 sts to holder, cast on 2 sts, k last 5 sts—12 sts. Knit 6 rnds. Bind off purlwise. Slip 19 sts back to larger dpns.

### Middle finger
**Next rnd** With G k5, sl next 10 sts to holder, cast on 2 sts, k last 4, pick up and knit 2 sts in ring finger's cast-on sts—13 sts. Knit 7 rnds. Bind off purlwise. Slip 10 sts back to larger dpns.

### Index finger
**Next rnd** With B k10, pick up and knit 2 sts in middle finger's cast-on sts—12 sts. Knit 7 rnds. Bind off purlwise.

### Thumb
Slip 11 thumb sts to larger dpns. With C k11, pick up and knit 2 sts in hand's cast-on sts—13 sts. Knit 5 rnds. Bind off purlwise.

# MUSIC PLAYER *Case*

## YOU'LL NEED:

### YARN
1¾oz/50g, 180yd/160m of any fingering weight variegated wool yarn

### NEEDLES
One set (4) size 4 (3.25mm) double-pointed needles (dpns) or *size to obtain gauge*

### ADDITIONAL MATERIALS
Size D/3 (3.25mm) crochet hook
Stitch marker
Tapestry needle
½"/1.5cm button with shank

### SIZE
One size. Sized for music players about 1.5"/3.8cm wide and 3–3½"/7.6–8.9cm tall.

### MEASUREMENTS
**Circumference** 3½"/9cm
**Length** 3½"/9cm

### GAUGE
28 sts and 40 rows to 4"/10cm over St st using size 4 (3.25mm) needles.
*Take time to check gauge.*

### CASE
Cast on 24 sts. Distribute sts evenly on 3 dpns. Join to work in rnds, taking care not to twist stitches. Place marker for end of rnd. **Next rnd** *K2, p2; rep from * around. Cont in k2, p2 rib for 4 more rnds. **Next rnd** Knit around. Continue in St st until piece measures 3½"/9cm. Distribute stitches onto 2 needles. Use 3-needle bind-off to close bottom opening. (See page 23 for 3-needle bind off instructions.)

### FINISHING
Sew button to center of one side at ½"/2cm down from top edge.
**Button loop**
With crochet hook, attach yarn to cast-on edge of case on side opposite marker. Ch 15, sl st in first st to form button loop.
**Earbud loop**
With crochet hook, attach yarn 1"/2.5cm below button. Ch 15, sl st in first st to form earbud loop.

Jack Deutsch

# COZY Wrap

Rose Callahan

## YOU'LL NEED:

### YARN
*Superwash Merino Cashmere* by Lion Brand Co. 17oz/482g, 1044yd/955m merino wool, nylon and cashmere blend in blossom

### NEEDLES
One pair size 10 (6mm) circular needle (at least 24"/60cm long) or *size to obtain gauge*

### ADDITIONAL MATERIALS
Yarn needle

### SIZE
One size. Also includes pillow pocket.

### MEASUREMENTS
Approximately 28" x 48"/71cm x 122cm

### GAUGE
16 sts and 24 rows to 4"/10 cm over pattern st using size 10 (6mm) needles.
*Take time to check gauge.*

### PATTERN STITCH
**Row 1 (RS)** P2, *sl1, k2, psso, p2; rep from * to end. **Row 2** *P1, yo, p1, k2; rep from * to end. **Row 3** P2, *k3, p2; rep from * to end. **Row 4** K2, *p3, k2; rep from * to end.
Rep rows 1–4 for pattern stitch.

### WRAP
Cast on 142 sts. Work in pattern stitch until piece measures 48"/122cm, ending with a pattern row 4. Bind off.
**Pillow Pocket**
Cast on 57 sts. Work in pattern stitch until pocket measures 9"/23cm, ending with a pattern row 4. Work 3 rows in k1, p1 ribbing. Bind off in rib.

### FINISHING
With right sides facing, sew on pocket to the center of the bottom edge of the wrap. Make sure to leave ribbed side open for turning. Fold wrap into thirds lengthwise and then widthwise and stuff into pillow pocket while turning pocket right side out.

# SEED & RIB Cowl

Rose Callahan

## YOU'LL NEED:

### YARN
3½oz/100g, 190yd/170m of any worsted weight wool yarn

### NEEDLES
One size 9 (5.5mm) circular needle, 24"/60cm long *or size to obtain gauge*

### ADDITIONAL MATERIALS
Stitch markers

## SIZE
One size. Sized for adult woman.

## MEASUREMENTS
**Circumference (rib)** 24"/61cm
**Circumference (widest point)** 26"/66cm
**Width** 8¾"/22cm

## GAUGE
16 sts and 24 rnds to 4"/10cm over St st, using size 9 (5.5mm) needles.
*Take time to check gauge.*

## STITCH GLOSSARY
**K1, p1 rib** (over an even number of sts)
**Rnd 1** *K1, p1; rep from * around.
**Rnd 2** K the knit sts, and p the purl sts.
Rep rnd 2 for k1, p1 rib.

**Seed stitch** (over an even number of sts)
**Rnd 1** *K1, p1; rep from * around.
**Rnd 2** P the knit sts and k the purl sts.
Rep rnd 2 for seed st.

## COWL
Cast on 96 sts, pm and join being careful not to twist sts. Work 4 rnds in k1, p1 rib. *K 5 rnds. Work 5 rnds in seed st; rep from * until there are 5 seed st bands. K 5 rnds. Work 5 rnds in k1, p1 rib. Bind off.

# CABLED Cowl

Jenny Acheson

## YOU'LL NEED:

### YARN [4]
17½oz/500g, 550yd/510m of any worsted weight wool blend yarn

### NEEDLES
Size 10 (6mm) circular needle, 24"/60cm length or *size to obtain gauge*

### ADDITIONAL MATERIALS
Cable needle, stitch markers

## SIZE
One size. Sized for adult woman.

## MEASUREMENTS
- **Width** 12"/30.5cm
- **Circumference** 40"/101.5cm

## GAUGE
14 sts and 16 rows to 4"/10cm over St st using size 10 (6mm) needle. *Take time to check gauge*

## STITCH GLOSSARY
**6-st LC (Left Cross)** Sl 3 sts to cn and hold to *front*, k3, k3 from cn.

## SCARF
Cast on 96 sts. Pm for beg of rnds. Join, being careful not to twist sts on needle.
**Beg rib**
**Rnd 1** For front work as foll: p3, [k3, p2] 5 times, k1, p3, k6, p3, k1, [p2, k2] 5 times, p3; pm, for back, work as foll: [k3, p2] twice, k28, [p2, k3] twice.
**Rnds 2–20** Knit the k sts and purl the p sts.
**Beg cable pat**
**Rnd 1** For front work as foll: p3, [k3, p2] 5 times, k1, p3, 6-st LC, p3, k1, [p2, k2] 5 times, p3, sl marker, for back, work as foll: [k3, p2] twice, k28, [p2, k3] twice.
**Rnds 2–8** Knit the k sts and purl the p sts.
Rep rnds 1–8 for 16 times more.
Work rib rnd 1 same as beg of scarf for 20 rnds. Bind off loosely in rib.

## FINISHING
Block lightly to measurements, centering front over back. Place scarf on work surface, front facing up. To form twist in scarf, bring cast-on and bound-off ends tog, then twist one end so back is facing up. Sew cast-on and bound-off ends tog.

# FELTED Needle Cases

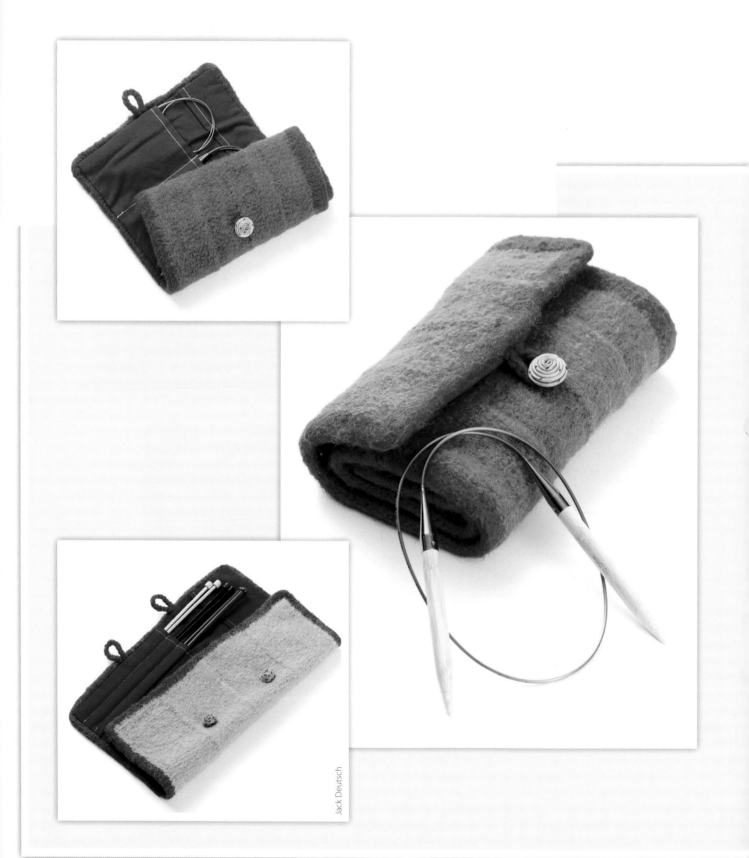

Jack Deutsch

# YOU'LL NEED:

## YARN (4)

### Straight needle case
7oz/200g, 260yd/240m of any worsted weight wool yarn in green (A)
3½oz/100g, 130yd/120m in magenta (B)
1yd/1m fabric for lining
Two 1"/25mm buttons

### Circular needle case
7oz/200g, 260yd/240m of any worsted weight wool yarn in orange (C)
3½oz/100g, 130yd/120m in red (D)
½yd/.5m fabric for lining
One 1"/25mm button

## NEEDLES
One pair size 9 (5.5mm) needles, or *size to obtain gauge*

## ADDITIONAL MATERIALS
Size G/6 (4mm) crochet hook
Sewing needle, matching thread, sewing machine

## SIZE
One size for straight needles, one size for circular needles.

## MEASUREMENTS
**Straight needle case**
**Before felting** 19½"/50cm wide by 21½"/55.5cm long
**After felting** 16"/40.5cm square
**Circular needle case**
**Before felting** 27½"/70.5cm wide by 13"/33cm high
**After felting** 23"/58.5cm wide by 9"/23cm high

## GAUGE
16 sts and 22 rows to 4"/10cm over St st, using size 9 (5.5mm) needles before felting. *Take time to check gauge.*

## STITCH GLOSSARY
### Crocheted edging
**Rnd 1** With RS facing, *work along cast-on edge and sl st in each st, work along side edge and sl st skipping every third st; rep from * along bound-off edge and rem side edge.
**Rnd 2** Sc in each st around, working 3 sc in each corner st.
**Rnds 3 and 4** Sl st in each st around.

## STRAIGHT NEEDLE CASE
With A, cast on 79 sts. Work [30 rows St st, 30 rows rev St st] twice. Bind off.
### Loops (make 2)
With B and crochet hook, chain for 4"/10cm. Fasten off, tie ends together.
### Edging
With B work crocheted edging around piece.
### Felting
Felt all pieces in washing machine. Tumble dry on high. Block with steam to shape.
### Lining
Cut fabric to 29½"/75cm by 17"/43cm. Fold under and press ½"/1cm hem along both short edges. Topstitch across hem at ³⁄₈"/1cm from folded edges. With topstitching on RS, fold one hemmed edge down 4"/10cm for top pocket, fold other edge up 8½"/21.5cm for lower pocket, adjusting to your felted piece if necessary. Fold under and press ½"/1cm hem along side edges. On lower pocket, sew vertical lines for channels as follows: 6 channels, each ⁷⁄₈"/2.2cm wide; 4 channels, each 1⅛"/2.5cm wide; and 3 channels, each 1½"/4cm wide. Pin lining to felted piece. Pin loops along one side edge, between lining and felted piece, centering 5"/12.5cm apart. Hand-stitch lining in place, covering loop ends. Fold in thirds, with loops on top. Sew buttons in place to correspond to loops.

## CIRCULAR NEEDLE CASE
With C, cast on 111 sts. Work [18 rows St st, 18 rows reverse St st] twice. Bind off.
### Loop
With D and crochet hook, chain for 4"/10cm. Fasten off, tie ends together.
### Edging
With D, work crocheted edging around piece.
### Felting
Felt all pieces in washing machine. Tumble dry on high. Block with steam to shape.
### Lining
Cut fabric to 24"/61cm by 17"/43cm. Fold under and press ½"/1cm hem along both long edges. Topstitch across hem at ³⁄₈"/1cm from fold edges. With topstitching on RS, fold one hemmed edge down 2"/5cm for top pocket, fold other edge up 5"/12.5cm for lower pocket, adjusting to your felted piece if necessary. Fold under and press ½"/1.5cm hem along side edges. On lower pocket, sew 5 vertical lines for pockets, each 3½"/9.5 cm apart. Pin lining to felted piece. Pin loop to center of one side edge, between lining and felted piece. Hand-stitch lining in place, covering loop ends. Roll up needle holder with loop on top. Sew button in place to correspond to loop.

# QUITE A Handful

Marcus Tullis

## YOU'LL NEED:

### YARN
**Mittens D, E, and H (3)**
3½oz/100g, 220yd/200m of any dk weight wool yarn

**Mittens A, C, and I (4)**
3½oz/100g, 220yd/200m of any worsted weight wool yarn

**Mittens B, F and G (5)**
3½oz/100g, 220yd/200m of any bulky weight wool yarn

### NEEDLES
**Mittens D, E, and H**
One set (5) size 6 (4mm) double-pointed needles (dpns) or *size to obtain gauge*
**Mittens A, C, and I**
One set (5) size 8 (5mm) dpns or *size to obtain gauge*
**Mittens B, F and G**
One set (5) size 10 (6mm) dpns or *size to obtain gauge*

### ADDITIONAL MATERIALS
**All Mittens**
Stitch markers and holder

A

B

C

D

E

F

G

H

I

## SIZE
Sizes vary. Mittens range in size from child to adult.

## MEASUREMENTS
**Palm** 9 (7½, 6)"/23 (19, 15)cm
**Length** 11½ (9½, 7)"/29 (24, 17.5)cm

## GAUGES
19 sts and 27 rnds to 4"/10cm over St st using DK weight wool and size 6 (4mm) needles.
16 sts and 24 rnds to 4"/10cm over St st using worsted weight wool and size 8 (5mm) needles.
14 sts and 17 rnds to 4"/10cm over St st using bulky weight wool and size 10 (6mm) needles.
*Take time to check your gauges.*

### Notes
**1** When changing colors in ribbing, always work first rnd of new color in St st.
**2** When making paired incs for the thumbs, make the first inc by knitting into the st below the next st on the L needle, make second inc by knitting into the st 2 sts below the st just knit.
**3** Some sizes work shaping differently on some rows. Look for the * in the pattern and on the chart.

## BASIC MITTEN PATTERN
Using chart on page 36 following column appropriate for your chosen size and yarn to fill in blanks, cast on __ sts. Divide on dpns, place marker and join for knitting in the round. Work in k2, p2 rib for __"/__cm. Change to St st and work even until piece measures __"/__ cm from ribbing.
**Next rnd** K__, M1, k__, M1, pm, k to end. Work 2 rnds even.
**Next rnd** K__, M1, k to marker, M1, sl m, k to end. Work 2 rnds even.
Rep last 3 rnds __ times.
**Next rnd** K__, cast on __, sl __ sts to holder,

k to end. Work 2 rnds even.
**Next rnd** * K__, ssk, k__, k2tog, k to end. Work 2 rnds even.
**Next rnd** * K__, ssk, k2tog, k to end. Work __ rnds even.
**Next rnd** [K2, k2tog, k__, ssk, pm, k__] twice. Work 2 rnds even.
**Next (dec) rnd** [K2, k2tog, k to 2 sts before marker, ssk, sl m, k __] twice. Work 1 rnd even.
Rep last 2 rnds __ times.
Rep dec rnd __ times.
Graft or sew rem sts together.

### Thumb
Pick up 1 st each side of thumb opening and __ sts along cast-on edge.
K across __ sts from holder.
**Next rnd** K1, ssk, k__, k2tog, k to end. Work 1 rnd.
**Next rnd** K1, ssk, k2tog, k around. K __ rnds even.
Cut yarn with an 8"/20.5cm tail, thread through rem sts and cinch tightly to close.

## MITTEN A
Shown in Woman's size.
### Materials
- 1¾oz/50g, 110yd/100m of worsted weight wool in color A (A) and color B (B)
- One set (5) size 8 (5mm) dpns *or size to obtain gauge*

**Mitten** (make 2)
Following Basic Mitten Pattern and chart for chosen size, begin mitten in A and work until ribbing is completed, finish with B. With A and using photo for reference, embroider flowers on backs of mittens with 5 lazy daisy petals and a large French knot center.

## MITTEN B
Shown in Woman's size.
### Materials
- 3½oz/100g,220yd/200m of bulky weight wool
- One set (5) size 10 (6mm) dpns *or size to obtain gauge*

**Mitten** (make 2)
Follow Basic Mitten Pattern and chart for chosen size.

## MITTEN C
Shown in Man's size.
### Materials
- 1¾oz/50g, 110yd/100m of worsted weight wool in color A (A) and color B (B)
- One set (5) size 8 (5mm) dpns *or size to obtain gauge*

**Mitten** (make 2)
Following Basic Mitten Pattern and chart for chosen size, begin mitten in A and work until 2 rnds completed, work in B until 17 rnds completed above ribbing, work [3 rnds in A, 2 rnds in B] four times, 3 rnds in A, finish in B. Work thumb to correspond.

## MITTEN D
Shown in Child's size.
### Materials
- 1¾oz/50g, 110yd/100m of DK weight wool in color A (A) and color B (B)
- One set (5) size 6 (5mm) dpns *or size to obtain gauge*

**Mitten** (make 2)
Following Basic Mitten Pattern and chart for chosen size, begin mitten in A and work until ribbing is completed, finish with B. With 2 strands of A, tapestry needle and chain st, embroider hearts on backs of mittens.

## MITTEN E
Shown in Man's size.
### Materials
- 1¾oz/50g, 110yd/100m of DK weight wool in color A (A) and color B (B)
- One set (5) size 6 (5mm) dpns *or size to obtain gauge*

**Mitten** (make 2)
Following Basic Mitten Pattern and chart for chosen size, begin mitten in A and work until 15 rnds completed over ribbing, work 2 rnds in B, 2 rnds in A, 19 rnds in B, 2 rnds

| | DK MAN | DK WOMAN | DK CHILD | WORSTED MAN | WORSTED WOMAN | WORSTED CHILD | BULKY MAN | BULKY WOMAN | BULKY CHILD |
|---|---|---|---|---|---|---|---|---|---|
| Cast on ___ sts | 44 | 36 | 28 | 36 | 32 | 24 | 32 | 28 | 20 |
| K2, p2 rib for ___"/___cm | 2¾/7 | 2¼/5.5 | 1¾/4.5 | 2¾/7 | 2¼/5.5 | 1¾/4.5 | 2¾/7 | 2¼/5.5 | 1¾/4.5 |
| St st for ___"/___cm | ¾/2 | ¾/2 | ½/1.5 | ¾/2 | ¾/2 | ½/1.5 | ¾/2 | ¾/2 | ½/1.5 |
| K___, M1, k___, M1, pm, k to end. Work 2 rnds even. | 20/4 | 16/4 | 13/3 | 16/4 | 14/4 | 11/3 | 15/4 | 13/4 | 9/3 |
| K___ M1, k to marker, M1, sl marker, k to end. Work 2 rnds even. | 20 | 16 | 13 | 16 | 14 | 11 | 15 | 13 | 9 |
| Rep last 3 rnds ___ times. | 4 | 3 | 2 | 3 | 3 | 2 | 3 | 2 | 1 |
| K___ cast on sl ___ sts to holder for thumb, k to end. Work 2 rnds even. | 21/6/12 | 17/6/10 | 14/5/7 | 17/6/10 | 15/6/10 | 12/5/7 | 16/5/9 | 14/5/7 | 10/5/5 |
| K___, ssk, k___, k2tog, k to end. Work 2 rnds even. | 21/2 | 17/2 | 14/1 | 17/2 | 15/2 | 12/1 | 16/1 | 14/1 | 10/1 |
| K___, ssk, k2tog, k to end. | 21 | 17 | 14* | 17 | 15 | 12* | 16* | 14* | 10* |
| Work ___ rnds even. | 16 | 12 | 7 | 16 | 12 | 8 | 5 | 4 | 1 |
| [K2, k2tog, k___, ssk, pm, k___] twice. Work 2 rnds even. | 14/2 | 10/2 | 7/1 | 10/2 | 8/2 | 5/1 | 9/1 | 7/1 | 3/1 |
| [K2, k2tog, k to 2 sts before marker, ssk, sl marker, k___] twice. (dec rnd). Work 1 rnd even. | 2 | 2 | 1 | 2 | 2 | 0 | 1 | 1 | 1 |
| Rep last 2 rnds ___ times. | 3 | 2 | 1 | 2 | 1 | 1 | 1 | 1 | 0 |
| Rep dec rnd ___ times. Graft rem sts tog. | 3 | 2 | 1 | 2 | 2 | 0 | 2 | 1 | 1 |
| THUMB: Pick up and k 1 st each side of thumb opening and ___ sts along cast-on edge. | 6 | 6 | 5 | 6 | 6 | 5 | 5 | 5 | 5 |
| K across ___ sts from holder. | 12 | 10 | 7 | 10 | 10 | 7 | 9 | 7 | 5 |
| K1, ssk, k___, k2tog, k to end. Work 1 rnd. K1, ssk, k2tog, k around. | 2 | 2 | 1 | 2 | 2 | 1 | 1 | 1 | 1 |
| K___ rnds even. Cut yarn, thread tail through rem sts and cinch tightly to close. | 12 | 8 | 6 | 10 | 7 | 6 | 7 | 5 | 3 |

* Work a sl 1, k2tog, psso instead of the ssk, k2tog

in A, 2 rnds in B, finish with A. Work thumb to correspond.

## MITTEN F
Shown in Child's size.
**Materials**
- 3½oz/100g, 220yd/200m of bulky weight wool
- One set (5) size 10 (6mm) dpns *or size to obtain gauge*

**Mitten** (make 2)
Follow Basic Mitten Pattern and chart for chosen size.

## MITTEN G
Shown in Man's size.
**Materials**
- 3½oz/100g, 220yd/200m of bulky weight wool
- One set (5) size 10 (6mm) dpns *or size to obtain gauge*

**Mitten** (make 2)
Follow Basic Mitten Pattern and chart for chosen size.

## MITTEN H
Shown in Woman's size.
**Materials**
- 1¾oz/50g, 110yd/100m of DK weight wool in color A (A) and color B (B)
- One set (5) size 8 (5mm) dpns *or size to obtain gauge*

**Mitten** (make 2)
Following Basic Mitten Pattern and chart for chosen size, begin mitten in A and work until 2 rnds completed, finish in B. With A, duplicate st Snowflake chart onto backs of mittens.

## MITTEN I
Shown in Child's size.
**Materials**
- 1¾oz/50g, 110yd/100m of worsted weight wool in color A (A) and color B (B)

- One set (5) size 6 (5mm) dpns *or size to obtain gauge*

**Mitten** (make 2)
Following Basic Mitten Pattern and chart for chosen size, begin mitten in A and work until rib is completed, work [4 rnds B and 1 rnd A] to end of mitten. Work thumb to correspond.

**SNOWFLAKE CHART**

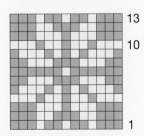

13
10
1

**COLOR KEY**
- ☐ Blue (A)
- ▧ Green (B)

Jack Deutsch

## YOU'LL NEED:

### YARN ❹

**Zebra**
5¼oz/150g, 420yd/390m of any worsted weight wool blend yarn in black (A)
3½oz/100g, 280yd/260m in natural (B)
Size 7 (4.25mm) needles or *size to obtain gauge*

**Horse**
7oz/200g, 550yd/510m of any worsted weight wool blend yarn in brown (C)
1¾oz/50g, 140yd/130m in black (A)
Size 7 (4.25mm) needles or *size to obtain gauge*

## ADDITIONAL MATERIALS
Polyester fiberfill
2  12"/30cm by 16"/41cm polyester pillow forms
Size G/6 (4mm) crochet hook
4½"/11.5cm flat 4-hole white buttons (2 per pillow)
Sewing needle and black thread

### SIZE
One size.

### MEASUREMENTS
**Body of each pillow** 12"/30cm wide by 16"/41cm long

### GAUGE
20 sts and 26 rows to 4"/10cm over St st using size 7 (4.25mm) needles.
*Take time to check gauge.*

### STITCH GLOSSARY
**Stripe pattern**
**Row 1 (RS)** With A knit.
**Row 2** With A purl.

**Row 3** With B knit.
**Row 4** With B purl.
Rep rows 1–4.

### ZEBRA PILLOW
**Body**
With A, cast on 120 sts. Work in St st and stripe pat for 16"/41cm, end with row 2 or 4. Bind off.
**Legs** (make 4)
With A, cast on 14 sts. Work in garter st for 1"/2.5cm. Join B, beg with row 2 of stripe pat and work even in St st until piece measures 6½"/16.5cm from beg. Bind off.
**Head** (make 2)
With A, cast on 14 sts. Work in St st and stripe pat, follow chart for shaping and nose. Bind off.

**Ears** (make 2)
With A, cast on 3 sts. Work in St st for 2 rows.
**Next (inc) row** K1, M1, k to last st, M1, k1—5 sts.
**Next row** Purl.
Rep last 2 rows once more—7 sts. Work 4 rows even.
**Next (dec) row** Ssk, k to last 2 sts, k2tog—5 sts.
**Next row** Purl.
Rep last 2 rows twice more—1 st. Fasten off.

## HORSE PILLOW
### Body
With C, cast on 120 sts. Work in St st for 16"/41cm. Bind off.
### Legs (make 4)
With A, cast on 14 sts. Work in garter st for 1"/2.5cm. With C, work even in St st until piece measures 6½"/16.5cm from beg. Bind off.
### Head (make 2)
With C, cast on 14 sts. Work in St st, follow chart for shaping and nose. Bind off.
### Ears (make 2)
With C, cast on 3 sts. Work in St st for 2 rows.
**Next (inc) row** K1, M1, k to last st, M1, k1—5 sts.
**Next row** Purl.
Rep last 2 rows once more—7 sts. Work 4 rows even.
**Next (dec) row** Ssk, k to last 2 sts, k2tog—5 sts.
**Next row** Purl.

Rep last 2 rows twice more—1 st. Fasten off.

## FINISHING
Block body piece to measurements. Fold legs in half lengthwise with RS tog, sew closed leaving cast-on edges open. Turn RS out.
Place both head pieces with RS tog, sew closed leaving bound-off edge open. Turn RS out; attach buttons for eyes as indicated on chart. Fold ears in half and attach to head as indicated on chart. Stuff with fiberfill. Sew rem edge closed.
Fold body in half widthwise with RS tog, zebra's stripes held vertically. Mark fold line for top of pillow and unfold to lay flat with RS facing. Position head at fold line, pointing inward. Allowing for ½"/.5cm seam, position 2 legs at each end of bottom edge, also pointing inward. Refold body with RS tog, head and legs are inside. Sew one side seam closed to attach head and bottom seam to attach legs. Turn body RS out, insert pillow form. Sew rem side seam.
### Mane
Cut forty 10"/25.5cm strands of A. With crochet hook, begin at ears and pull each strand through to make fringe working along top edge of head and halfway across back. Trim mane to 4"/10cm.

## TAIL
### Zebra
Cut three 15"/38cm strands of A. With crochet hook, pull all strands through top corner, opposite head. Fold strands in half and braid together, making one tail strand. Make a knot, leaving 2"/5cm loose at end.
### Horse
Cut twelve 17"/43cm strands of A. Fold strands in half. With crochet hook, pull all strands through top corner, opposite head to make fringe. Trim to 8"/20cm.

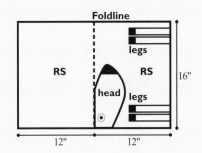

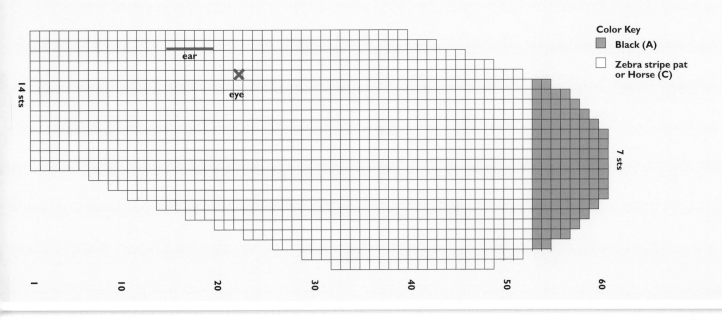

# MY Notes